contents

NZ, Canada, US and UK readers
Please note that Australian cup and
spoon measurements are metric.
A conversion chart appears on page 63.

LUNCH ON THE GO...

Very few of us relish the idea of packing lunch to take to work — another dreary part of the yet-another-chore-to-do-in-the-morning syndrome. And we'd be hard-pressed to truthfully say that we've seldom savoured the soggy sanger anyway by the time lunchtime rolls around. Read on for some top tips on how to bypass some of the stress of the morning rush hour yet still arrive at your midday destination with a fresh and appealing homemade lunch. Some of the ideas in this book are great for school lunchboxes, but most of them are for adults.

ORGANISE WEDNESDAY'S LUNCH THE SUNDAY BEFORE

It might be a bit of a drag at the time, but preparing some components for a week's-worth of lunches on Sunday afternoon will be extremely appreciated come Wednesday morning. Buy fresh bread on Sunday, slice if need-be and freeze it; poach a chicken breast and chop it; roast a small piece of scotch fillet or a few lamb fillets; make an oven-baked vegetable frittata and cut it into squares; par-boil small amounts of lentils and beans; or hard-boil a few eggs. Don't overdo it though; unlike diamonds, cooked foods don't last forever — not even five days. Organise yourself: if you know what you're going to make for dinner on successive nights, think about what, if anything, you can make extra of to take for lunch later in the week. Make a mini version of the lasagne you're having on Tuesday and reheat it in the microwave oven on Wednesday at work; freeze an individual container of Saturday night's minestrone and defrost it in your office fridge on Thursday morning. What you expend on planning and organising on the weekend, you make up threefold in time on weekday mornings. Have a go and see if you're not converted.

PLASTIC IS YOUR FRIEND.

• Take sandwich filling, bread and salad topping to work in individual containers or snap-lock bags; refrigerate until lunchtime; assemble just when you want to eat. No more limp lettuce, dry tomato or bread that falls apart under the weight of it all: when you really want a just-made sandwich, you've got it.

• Freeze several cup-size portions of homemade stock in two-cup capacity plastic containers. On the day you want soup for lunch, take a single container, still frozen, to work with you, along with whatever other soup contents you want, in other containers. The stock will have thawed by noon when you'll add to it all the other ingredients, reheating the whole lot in a microwave oven.

• Never pack a dressed salad or a sauced pasta. Keep the greens, croutons and dressing in separate containers (pour the dressing into a snap-lock bag then throw it away to avoid having to wash a greasy container). Ditto the pasta shells and their sun-dried tomato sauce: the pasta will just suck up the sauce if they're forced to nestle together in a single container for several hours.

tuna and sweet corn sandwich

½ x 185g can tuna
   in springwater,
      drained, flaked
2 tablespoons canned
   sweet corn kernels,
      rinsed, drained
1 tablespoon mayonnaise
2 slices multigrain bread
¼ lebanese cucumber,
   sliced thinly

1 At home, combine tuna, corn and mayonnaise in small container.
2 At lunchtime, spread tuna mixture on one slice of bread. Top with cucumber and remaining slice of bread.

makes 1 sandwich
per sandwich 9.7g total fat (1.7g saturated fat); 1379kJ (330 cal); 34.4g carbohydrate; 24.4g protein; 3g fibre

cheese and vegie sandwich

2 tablespoons coarsely
   grated cheddar cheese
2 tablespoons coarsely
   grated carrot
2 tablespoons coarsely
   grated celery
1 tablespoon sour cream
2 slices wholemeal bread

1 At home, combine cheese, carrot, celery and sour cream in small container.
2 At lunchtime, spread vegie mixture over one slice of bread; top with another slice of bread.

makes 1 sandwich
per sandwich 16.2g total fat (9.6g saturated); 1275kJ (305 cal); 26.1g carbohydrate; 11.5g protein; 6.2g fibre

roast beef and horseradish cream on focaccia

1 small focaccia
2 teaspoons horseradish cream
50g sliced roast beef
¼ cup thickly sliced char-grilled capsicum
20g baby rocket leaves

1 At home, split focaccia in half horizontally; spread horseradish cream on cut-side of one half of focaccia.
2 At lunchtime, top horseradish cream with beef, capsicum, rocket and remaining focaccia.

makes 1 focaccia
per focaccia 12.4g total fat (2.8g saturated fat); 2270kJ (543 cal); 77.7g carbohydrate; 28.7g protein; 4.7g fibre

tuna salad sandwich

425g can tuna in brine,
    drained, flaked
½ small red capsicum (75g),
    chopped finely
1 green onion, sliced thinly
10 pitted kalamata olives,
    chopped finely
½ trimmed celery stalk
    (50g), chopped finely
1 teaspoon finely chopped
    flat-leaf parsley
½ cup (150g) mayonnaise
6 slices white bread
90g green oak lettuce

1 At home, combine tuna, capsicum, onion, olives, celery, parsley and mayonnaise in medium bowl.
2 At lunchtime, spread a third of the tuna mixture on one slice of bread; top with lettuce and another slice of bread. Repeat with remaining mixture, bread and lettuce.

makes 3 sandwiches
per sandwich 20.4g total fat (3.2g saturated fat); 1940kJ (464 cal); 38.3g carbohydrate; 31.9g protein; 2.8g fibre
tip Make the filling in advance; store in an airtight container in the refrigerator for up to three days.

chicken salad sandwich

1½ cups (240g) finely
    chopped cooked chicken
4 green onions, sliced thinly
2 tablespoons pecans,
    chopped finely
½ trimmed celery stalk (50g)
    chopped finely
¼ cup (75g) mayonnaise
6 slices wholemeal bread
60g rocket

1 At home, combine chicken, onion, nuts, celery and mayonnaise in medium bowl.
2 At lunchtime, spread a third of the chicken mixture on one slice of bread; top with rocket and another slice of bread. Repeat with remaining mixture, bread and rocket.

makes 3 sandwiches
per sandwich 19.2g total fat (3.2g saturated fat); 1668kJ (399 cal); 31.1g carbohydrate; 25.4g protein; 2.9g fibre
tip Make the filling in advance; store in an airtight container in the refrigerator for up to three days.

lamb, tabbouleh and hummus on pitta

1 pocket pitta bread
1 tablespoon hummus
¼ cup tabbouleh
50g sliced roast lamb
20g baby rocket leaves

1 At lunchtime, cut pitta in half; separate bread to form a pocket. Spread hummus on inside of each pitta. Place equal amounts of tabbouleh, lamb and rocket inside each pitta.

makes 1 pitta
per pitta 13.1g total fat (4.2g saturated fat); 1237kJ (296 cal); 23.4g carbohydrate; 21.2g protein; 4.3g fibre

egg salad sandwich

5 hard-boiled eggs,
   chopped finely
2 medium tomatoes (300g),
   chopped coarsely
¼ cup (75g) mayonnaise
6 slices white bread
60g mesclun

1 At home, combine egg, tomato and mayonnaise in medium bowl.
2 At lunchtime, top bread with a third of the mesclun, egg mixture and another slice of bread. Repeat with remaining mixture, mesclun and bread.

makes 3 sandwiches
per sandwich 19g total fat (4g saturated fat); 1517kJ (363 cal); 31.2g carbohydrate; 16.9g protein; 2.5g fibre
tip Make the filling in advance; store in an airtight container in the refrigerator for up to three days.

pea, ricotta, mint and spinach sandwich

¾ cup (90g) frozen peas
¾ cup (150g) ricotta
¼ cup (60ml) lemon juice
¼ cup finely chopped
   fresh mint
6 slices soy and
   linseed bread
60g baby spinach leaves

1 At home, boil, steam or microwave peas until tender; drain. Cool, then lightly crush peas with fork. Combine pea mash with ricotta, juice and mint.
2 At lunchtime, spread a third of the pea mixture on one slice of bread; top with spinach and another slice of bread. Repeat with remaining mixture, remaining bread and spinach.

makes 3 sandwiches
per sandwich 8.5g total fat (3.9g saturated fat); 995kJ (238 cal); 26g carbohydrate; 13.8g protein; 6.8g fibre
tip Make the filling in advance; store in an airtight container in the refrigerator for up to three days.

smoked trout salad roll

50g flaked smoked trout
1 tablespoon sour cream
1 tablespoon finely chopped cornichons
1 tablespoon finely chopped fresh dill
1 tablespoon lemon juice
1 wholemeal bread roll

1 At home, combine trout, sour cream, cornichons, dill and lemon juice in small container.
2 At lunchtime, split roll in half horizontally; spread one half with trout mixture. Top with remaining half of roll.

makes 1 roll
per roll 13.2g total fat (6.1g saturated fat); 1576kJ (377 cal); 42.3g carbohydrate; 21.4g protein; 5.2g fibre
tip Make the filling in advance; store in an airtight container in the refrigerator for up to two days.

turkey and cream cheese roll-ups

1 piece lavash bread
1 tablespoon spreadable cream cheese
3 slices (65g) smoked turkey
3 cheese slices
3 iceberg lettuce leaves
1 small (60g) egg tomato, sliced thinly

1 At lunchtime, spread bread with cream cheese. Place turkey, cheese, lettuce and tomato on bread; roll tightly then cut in half.

makes 2 roll-ups
per roll-up 13.9g total fat (8g saturated fat); 1187kJ (284 cal); 19g carbohydrate; 20g protein; 1.9g fibre

hummus and cucumber sandwich

2 slices country loaf bread
1 tablespoon hummus
¼ lebanese cucumber (30g),
   sliced thinly

1 At lunchtime, spread 1 slice of bread with hummus; top with cucumber and remaining bread.

makes 1 sandwich
per sandwich 5g total fat (0.9g saturated fat); 769kJ (184 cal); 27.6g carbohydrate; 6.8g protein; 3.8g fibre

chicken, avocado and cream cheese sandwich

¼ cup (40g) coarsely
   chopped cooked chicken
¼ small avocado (50g),
   chopped coarsely
1 teaspoon lemon juice
1 tablespoon spreadable
   cream cheese
2 slices multigrain bread
60g mesclun

1 At lunchtime, combine chicken, avocado and juice in small bowl.
2 Spread cream cheese on 1 slice of bread; top with chicken mixture, mesclun and remaining bread.

makes 1 sandwich
per sandwich 21g total fat (7.3g saturated fat); 1438kJ (344 cal); 25.9g carbohydrate; 13g protein; 2.4g fibre

chicken burritos

1¼ cups (200g) coarsely chopped cooked chicken
¼ cup (75g) mayonnaise
¼ cup (60g) sour cream
1 cup (60g) finely shredded lettuce
2 small tomatoes (180g), chopped finely
½ cup (60g) coarsely grated cheddar
3 x 20cm flour tortillas

1 At home, combine chicken, mayonnaise and sour cream in medium bowl.
2 At lunchtime, divide chicken mixture, lettuce, tomato and cheese among tortillas; roll securely to enclose filling. Cut tortillas in half.

makes 6 half-burritos
per half-burrito 15g total fat (6g saturated fat); 1007kJ (241 cal); 15.6g carbohydrate; 11.2g protein; 1.5g fibre
tip Make the filling in advance; store in an airtight container in the refrigerator for up to two days.

ham, tomato and avocado open sandwich

1 medium egg tomato (75g), cut in half
2 teaspoons brown sugar
2 slices ciabatta
¼ small avocado (50g), sliced
50g shaved ham

1 At home, a day ahead, preheat oven to moderate (180°C/160°C fan forced).
2 Place tomato, cut-side up, on oven tray, sprinkle with sugar; cook, uncovered, for 20 minutes. Cool, cover, refrigerate.
3 At lunchtime, toast ciabatta; divide avocado, ham and tomato between slices. Sprinkle with pepper, if desired.

makes 2 slices
per slice 5.8g total fat (1.3g saturated fat); 686kJ (164 cal); 19.8g carbohydrate; 8g protein; 1.8g fibre

prawn and lime mayonnaise open sandwich

2 tablespoons mayonnaise
2 teaspoons finely
  chopped fresh dill
1 tablespoon lime juice
2 slices ciabatta
10g baby rocket leaves
8 cooked small prawns

1 At home, make lime mayonnaise by combining mayonnaise, dill and lime juice.
2 At lunchtime, toast ciabatta; divide rocket, prawns and mayonnaise mixture between slices.

makes 2 slices
per slice 7.2g total fat (0.9g saturated fat); 832kJ (199 cal); 19.5g carbohydrate; 13.6g protein; 1.2g fibre

smoked chicken and mango chutney open sandwich

2 slices ciabatta
2 teaspoons mayonnaise
100g thinly sliced
  smoked chicken
10g mesclun
1 tablespoon
  mango chutney

1 At lunchtime, toast ciabatta; spread mayonnaise over both slices.
2 Divide chicken, mesclun and chutney between slices.

makes 2 slices
per slice 6g total fat (1.3g saturated fat); 853kJ (204 cal); 22g carbohydrate; 15.4g protein; 1.4g fibre

vegetable frittata

2 medium potatoes (400g), peeled, cut into 1cm slices
1 medium kumara (400g), peeled, cut into 1cm slices
10 eggs
½ cup (125ml) cream
1 cup (80g) coarsely grated parmesan
½ cup (60g) coarsely grated cheddar
50g baby rocket leaves
2 tablespoons thinly sliced fresh basil

1 At home, a day ahead, preheat oven to moderate
(180°C/160°C fan forced). Oil deep 19cm-square cake pan;
line base and sides with baking paper, extending paper 5cm
above edges.
2 Boil, steam or microwave potato and kumara, separately,
until just tender; drain.
3 Meanwhile, whisk eggs, cream and both cheeses in large jug.
4 Layer potato slices in cake pan; top with rocket, kumara then
basil. Carefully pour egg mixture over vegetables.
5 Bake frittata, covered, 45 minutes or until browned. Cool to
room temperature, then cut into triangles; refrigerate until cold.

serves 4
per serving 38.5g total fat (20.3g saturated fat); 2403kJ
(575 cal); 25.4g carbohydrate; 32.8g protein; 3.2g fibre
tips The frittata can be eaten cold or warm.
Store frittata slices, in an airtight container, in the refrigerator
for up to three days.

chicken caesar salad

3 bacon rashers (210g), rind removed, chopped coarsely
4 hard-boiled eggs, quartered
2 cups (320g) coarsely shredded cooked chicken
700g cos lettuce, sliced thickly
½ cup (125ml) caesar salad dressing
½ cup (40g) shaved parmesan

1 At home, cook bacon in heated small non-stick frying
pan until crisp; drain on absorbent paper. Place bacon
in large bowl with egg, chicken and lettuce.
2 At lunchtime, add dressing and cheese to salad; toss
gently to combine.

serves 4
per serving 35.8g total fat (8.6g saturated fat); 2040kJ
(488 cal); 3.5g carbohydrate; 38.4g protein; 3.7g fibre
tip Divide this salad among family members for lunch,
or keep, covered, in the refrigerator, for up to three days.

lentil, beetroot and rocket salad

½ cup cooked brown lentils
½ cup drained canned
 baby beetroot halves
1 tablespoon
 balsamic vinegar
1 teaspoon olive oil
1½ cups baby rocket leaves
30g crumbled fetta

1 At home, combine lentils and beetroot. Combine vinegar and oil; toss dressing with lentil mixture.
2 At lunchtime, serve lentils and beetroot on rocket; top with cheese.

serves 1
per serving 12.6g total fat (5.3g saturated fat); 1037kJ (248 cal); 18.8g carbohydrate; 15g protein; 6.9g fibre

tuna salad

125g can sliced tuna in
 springwater, drained
1½ teaspoons rinsed
 drained baby capers
⅓ cup halved cherry
 tomatoes
3 teaspoons fresh dill sprigs
1 tablespoon lemon juice
1 teaspoon olive oil
2 cups baby spinach leaves

1 At home, combine tuna, capers, tomatoes, dill, juice and oil; toss salad.
2 At lunchtime, add spinach to salad.

serves 1
per serving 7g total fat (1.5g saturated fat); 694kJ (166 cal); 2.5g carbohydrate; 22.3g protein; 2.8g fibre

rice and corn salad

1 cup (200g) white long-grain rice
1 cup (250ml) chicken stock
125g can corn kernels, drained
½ cup (75g) semi-dried tomatoes, halved
¼ cup (40g) pine nuts, toasted
4 green onions, sliced thinly
¼ cup (30g) green olives, sliced
1 cup coarsely chopped fresh basil
mustard dressing
¼ cup (60ml) olive oil
1 tablespoon lemon juice
1 teaspoon wholegrain mustard
½ clove garlic, crushed

1 At home, a day ahead, place rice in large sieve, rinse under cold water until water runs clear.
2 Bring stock to a boil in medium saucepan; add rice, reduce heat, simmer, covered, over low heat about 10 minutes or until the rice is just tender and all the liquid is absorbed. Fluff rice with fork; cool.
3 Meanwhile combine ingredients for mustard dressing in screw-top jar; shake well. Store in refrigerator.
4 Place cooled rice, corn, tomato, nuts, onion, olives and basil in large bowl. Store, covered, in refrigerator.
5 At lunchtime, add mustard dressing to rice and corn salad; toss gently to combine.

serves 3
per serving 30.9g total fat (3.7g saturated fat); 2642kJ (632 cal); 76.2g carbohydrate; 12.1g protein; 7.4g fibre
tip Salad and dressing can be divided into individual portions. Keep, covered, in the refrigerator for up to three days.

mini pea frittatas

6 eggs
½ cup (125ml) cream
½ cup (60g) grated cheddar
¼ cup chopped fresh chives
2 tablespoons chopped fresh basil
½ cup (60g) frozen peas

1 At home, a day ahead, preheat oven to moderately slow (170°C/150°C fan forced). Lightly grease eight holes (⅓-cup/80ml) of a muffin pan.
2 Whisk eggs and cream in medium bowl. Stir in cheese, herbs and half of the peas. Pour egg mixture into pan holes.
3 Bake frittatas 15 minutes. Sprinkle frittatas with remaining peas; bake further 15 minutes or until egg is just set. Stand frittatas 5 minutes before turning out. Refrigerate until cold.

makes 8
per frittata 13.3g total fat (7.3g saturated fat); 640kJ (153 cal); 1.1g carbohydrate; 7.7g protein; 0.5g fibre
tip Frittatas can be eaten cold or warm.
Store frittatas, in an airtight container, in the refrigerator for up to three days.

chicken and corn soup

125g can creamed corn
½ cup shredded
    cooked chicken
1 tablespoon soy sauce
½ teaspoon sambal oelek
375ml carton salt-reduced
    chicken stock
2 tablespoons fresh
    flat-leaf parsley leaves

1 At home, combine corn, chicken, soy sauce and sambal.

2 At lunchtime, place corn mixture and stock in medium microwave-safe bowl. Cook, uncovered, on HIGH (100%) in microwave oven about 2 minutes or until hot. Sprinkle with parsley.

serves 1
per serving 8.6g total fat (2.7g saturated fat); 1200kJ (287 cal); 24.5g carbohydrate; 27.5g protein; 4.8g fibre

french onion soup

2 teaspoons olive oil
1 medium brown onion
    (150g), sliced thinly
2 teaspoons brown sugar
375ml carton salt-reduced
    beef stock
1 teaspoon coarsely
    chopped fresh chives

1 At home, a day ahead, heat oil in small frying pan, add onion; cook, stirring, until onion softens. Add sugar; cook, stirring occasionally, about 10 minutes or until onion caramelises.

2 At lunchtime, place onion mixture and stock in medium microwave-safe bowl. Cook, uncovered, on HIGH (100%) in microwave oven about 2 minutes or until hot. Sprinkle with chives.

serves 1
per serving 10g total fat (1.7g saturated fat); 757kJ (181 cal); 16.7g carbohydrate; 6.6g protein; 2g fibre

chicken and vegetable soup

1 cup (250ml) water
1.25 litres (5 cups) chicken stock
2 trimmed celery stalks (200g), sliced thinly
2 medium carrots (240g), chopped finely
1 large potato (300g), chopped finely
150g snow peas, trimmed, chopped coarsely
3 green onions, sliced thinly
310g can corn kernels, drained
3 cups (480g) coarsely shredded barbecued chicken

1 At home, a day ahead, place the water and stock in large saucepan; bring to a boil. Add celery, carrot and potato; return to a boil. Reduce heat; simmer, covered, about 10 minutes or until vegetables are just tender.

2 Add snow peas, onion and corn to soup; cook, covered, 2 minutes. Cool, stir in chicken.

3 At lunchtime, place soup in medium microwave-safe bowl; cook, uncovered, on HIGH (100%) in microwave oven about 2 minutes or until hot.

serves 4
per serving 8.5g total fat (2.4g saturated fat); 1317kJ (315 cal); 31.6g carbohydrate; 27.9g protein; 7g fibre
tip Freeze soup in individual portions.
You need one large barbecued chicken weighing about 900g for this recipe. Discard the skin and remove all the meat from the bones; using a fork, shred meat coarsely.

potato and kumara salad
with honey mustard dressing

4 medium potatoes (800g), unpeeled, chopped coarsely
1 medium kumara (400g), peeled, chopped coarsely
150g green beans, trimmed, sliced thickly
2 green onions, sliced thickly
honey mustard dressing
⅔ cup (200g) mayonnaise
1 tablespoon water
2 teaspoons honey
2 teaspoons wholegrain mustard

1 At home, a day ahead, boil, steam or microwave potato, kumara and beans, separately, until just tender; drain. Place potato and kumara in large bowl. Rinse beans under cold water; drain.
2 Meanwhile, whisk ingredients for honey mustard dressing in small bowl until combined.
3 Combine beans, onion and half of the dressing in bowl with potato and kumara; toss gently to combine.
4 At lunchtime, combine potato mixture with remaining honey mustard dressing.

serves 4
per serving 16.4g total fat (1.9g saturated fat); 1597kJ (382 cal); 50.6g carbohydrate; 7.6g protein; 6.8g fibre

chicken and peach salad

½ cup (80g) shredded barbecued chicken
1½ cups shredded chinese cabbage
¼ cup shredded fresh mint leaves
1 small peach (115g)
2 tablespoons lime juice
1 teaspoon olive oil

1 At home, combine chicken, cabbage and mint in
medium bowl.
2 At lunchtime, peel peach and cut into wedges; add to chicken
mixture. Combine juice and oil; toss dressing through salad.

serves 1
per serving 11g total fat (2.4g saturated fat); 957kJ (229 cal);
8.4g carbohydrate; 22.5g protein; 3.9g fibre

minestrone

1 tablespoon olive oil
1 small brown onion (80g), chopped finely
1 clove garlic, crushed
2 bacon rashers (140g), rind removed, chopped finely
1 trimmed celery stalk (100g), grated coarsely
2 medium carrots (240g), grated coarsely
400g can chopped tomatoes
2 cups (500ml) beef stock
1 litre (4 cups) water
½ cup (65g) short pasta
2 medium zucchini (240g), grated coarsely
300g can white beans, rinsed, drained
⅓ cup shredded fresh basil

1 At home, a day ahead, heat oil in large saucepan; cook onion, garlic, bacon and celery, stirring, about 5 minutes or until vegetables just soften.
2 Add carrot, undrained tomato, stock, the water and pasta; bring to a boil. Reduce heat; simmer, covered, about 5 minutes or until pasta is just tender. Stir in zucchini and beans; remove from heat, cool then refrigerate.
3 At lunchtime, place soup in medium microwave-safe bowl; cook, uncovered, on HIGH (100%) in microwave oven about 2 minutes or until hot. Stir in basil. Serve with toast, if desired.

serves 4
per serving 8.1g total fat (1.7g saturated fat); 928kJ (222 cal); 25.4g carbohydrate; 12.1g protein; 7.5g fibre
tips Freeze soup in individual portions.
Many varieties of already-cooked white beans are available canned, among them cannellini, butter and haricot beans; any of these is suitable for this soup.
You can use any small pasta for this recipe, such as little shells or small macaroni.

chickpea salad

½ cup rinsed, drained, canned chickpeas
1 lebanese cucumber (130g), chopped coarsely
½ small red onion (50g), sliced thinly
¼ cup (40g) seeded kalamata olives
⅓ cup fresh flat-leaf parsley leaves
¼ cup coarsely chopped yellow capsicum
1 small egg tomato (90g), chopped
2 tablespoons tzatziki
dressing
1 tablespoon lemon juice
1 teaspoon olive oil
¼ teaspoon finely chopped lemon rind
¼ teaspoon ground cumin

1 At home, combine chickpeas, cucumber, onion, olives, parsley, capsicum and tomato in medium bowl.
2 Combine ingredients for dressing in screw-top jar; shake well.
3 At lunchtime, toss dressing with salad. Top with tzatziki.

serves 1
per serving 12.6g total fat (3g saturated fat); 1162kJ (278 cal); 29.3g carbohydrate; 11.9g protein; 9.8g fibre

thai beef salad

500g beef rump steak
60g bean thread noodles
1 lebanese cucumber (130g), seeded, sliced thinly
100g cherry tomatoes, quartered
1 small red capsicum (150g), sliced thinly
3 green onions, sliced thinly
⅓ cup firmly packed fresh coriander leaves
⅓ cup firmly packed fresh mint leaves
thai dressing
¼ cup (60ml) lemon juice
1 tablespoon fish sauce
1 tablespoon brown sugar
1 tablespoon peanut oil

1 At home, a day ahead, cook beef in heated oiled large
frying pan until browned both sides and cooked as desired.
Cover; stand 10 minutes, then slice beef thinly.
2 Meanwhile, place noodles in large heatproof bowl, cover
with boiling water, stand until just tender; drain into colander.
Using kitchen scissors, cut noodles into random lengths.
3 Combine ingredients for thai dressing in screw-top jar;
shake well.
4 Combine noodles with remaining ingredients in large bowl;
cover and refrigerate.
5 At lunchtime, add dressing to salad; toss gently to combine.

serves 4
per serving 13.1g total fat (4.6g saturated fat); 1166kJ (279 cal);
10.5g carbohydrate; 29.5g protein; 1.9g fibre
tip Divide this salad among family members for lunch, or keep,
covered, in the refrigerator, for up to three days.

mediterranean pasta salad

250g orecchiette
2 tablespoons drained sun-dried tomatoes, chopped coarsely
1 small red onion (100g), sliced thinly
1 small green capsicum (150g), sliced thinly
½ cup coarsely chopped fresh flat-leaf parsley
sun-dried tomato dressing
1 tablespoon sun-dried tomato pesto
1 tablespoon white wine vinegar
2 tablespoons olive oil

1 At home, a day ahead, cook pasta in large saucepan of
boiling water, uncovered, until just tender; drain. Rinse under
cold water; drain.
2 Meanwhile, combine ingredients for sun-dried tomato dressing
in screw-top jar; shake well.
3 Place pasta in large bowl with remaining ingredients; cover
and refrigerate.
4 At lunchtime, add dressing to salad; toss gently to combine.

serves 4
per serving 12g total fat (1.9g saturated fat); 1375kJ (329 cal);
46g carbohydrate; 8.8g protein; 3.7g fibre
tip Divide this salad among family members for lunch, or keep,
covered, in the refrigerator, for up to three days.

pumpkin soup

20g butter
1 medium white onion (150g), chopped finely
2 bacon rashers (140g), rind removed, chopped finely
750g piece butternut pumpkin, peeled, seeded, chopped
3½ cups (375ml) chicken stock

1 At home, a day ahead, melt butter in large saucepan, add onion and bacon; cook, stirring until onion is soft.
2 Add pumpkin and stock; bring to a boil. Reduce heat; simmer, uncovered, about 30 minutes or until pumpkin is soft. Cool pumpkin mixture before blending or processing in batches until smooth.
3 At lunchtime, place soup in medium microwave-safe bowl; cook, uncovered, on HIGH (100%) in microwave oven about 2 minutes or until hot.

serves 4
per serving 7.9g total fat (4.3g saturated fat); 660kJ (158 cal); 13.4g carbohydrate; 8.4g protein; 2.5g fibre
tip Soup can be frozen in individual portions.

risoni and spring vegetable soup

¼ cup (55g) risoni
2 green beans, sliced thinly
1 small carrot (70g), sliced thinly
375ml carton salt-reduced chicken or vegetable stock
1 tablespoon shredded fresh basil

1 At home, a day ahead, cook risoni in small saucepan
of boiling water, uncovered, until almost tender. Add
beans and carrot; cook, uncovered, 1 minute. Drain;
rinse under cold water, then drain again.
2 At lunchtime, place risoni mixture and stock in
medium microwave-safe bowl. Cook, uncovered, on
HIGH (100%) in microwave oven about 2 minutes or
until hot. Sprinkle with basil.

serves 1
per serving 2.2g total fat (0.9g saturated fat); 1007kJ
(241 cal); 43.7g carbohydrate; 11.1g protein; 3.9g fibre

thai chicken noodle soup

½ cup thinly sliced cooked chicken
1 teaspoon red curry paste
175g packet singapore noodles
375ml carton salt-reduced chicken stock
1 tablespoon coarsely chopped fresh coriander
½ green onion, sliced thinly

1 At home, combine chicken and curry paste.
2 At lunchtime, rinse noodles under hot water. Place noodles
in medium microwave-safe bowl with chicken mixture and stock.
Cook, uncovered, on HIGH (100%) in microwave oven about
2 minutes or until hot. Sprinkle with coriander and onion.

serves 1
per serving 5.2g total fat (1.3g saturated fat); 2140kJ (512 cal);
93.9g carbohydrate; 21.1g protein; 4.1g fibre

baked potato, ham
and cheese frittata

4 medium potatoes (800g)
4 eggs, beaten lightly
½ cup (90g) finely chopped leg ham
1 medium tomato (150g), chopped finely
2 green onions, sliced thinly
1 tablespoon finely chopped fresh flat-leaf parsley
1 cup (120g) coarsely grated cheddar

1 At home, a day ahead, preheat oven to moderate
(180°C/160°C fan-forced). Lightly grease shallow
1.5-litre (6 cup) ovenproof dish.
2 Grate potatoes coarsely; squeeze out excess water.
3 Combine potato, egg, ham, tomato, onion, parsley and
half of the cheese in medium bowl. Spread mixture into dish;
sprinkle with remaining cheese.
4 Bake, uncovered, about 40 minutes or until browned.
Cool to room temperature, then cut into squares; refrigerate
until cold.

serves 4
per serving 17.1g total fat (8.7g saturated fat); 1501kJ
(359 cal); 27.5g carbohydrate; 23.1g protein; 3.8g fibre
tip The frittata can be eaten cold or warm.
Store frittata slices, in an airtight container, in the refrigerator
for up to three days.

glossary

bacon rasher also known as slices of bacon, made from pork side, cured and smoked.

barbecue sauce a spicy, tomato-based sauce used to marinate, baste or as a condiment.

bean thread noodles also known as glass or cellophane noodles because they are transparent when cooked. White in colour, very delicate and fine; are available dried in various size bundles. Must be soaked to soften before use; using them deep-fried requires no pre-soaking.

bicarbonate of soda also known as baking soda.

butter use salted or unsalted (sweet) butter; 125g is equal to 1 stick butter.

butternut pumpkin used interchangeably with the word squash; butternut pumpkin is a member of the gourd family. It is pear-shaped with golden skin and orange flesh.

cabanossi a ready-to-eat sausage; also known as cabana.

capsicum also known as bell pepper or, simply, pepper. Seeds and membranes must be discarded before use.

cheese
  cheddar the most common cow-milk 'tasty' cheese; should be aged, hard and have a pronounced bite. For our lower-fat versions we used one with no more than 20% fat.
  fetta a crumbly textured goat or sheep-milk cheese with a sharp, salty taste.

jarlsberg a Norwegian cheese made from cow milk; has large holes and a mild, nutty taste.

mozzarella soft, spun-curd cheese. Has a low melting point and elastic texture.

parmesan also known as parmigiano, parmesan is a hard, grainy cow-milk cheese. The curd is salted in brine for a month before being aged for up to two years in humid conditions.

pizza cheese a commercial blend of varying proportions of processed grated mozzarella, cheddar and parmesan.

ricotta a soft, white, cow-milk cheese. Made from whey, a by-product of other cheese making, to which fresh milk and acid are added.

spreadable cream cheese available in glass jars at the supermarket; must be refrigerated after opening.

tasty matured cheddar; use an aged, strongly-flavoured, hard variety.

chinese cabbage also known as peking or napa cabbage, wong bok or petsai. Elongated in shape with pale green, crinkly leaves; it is the most common cabbage in South-East Asia.

cornichons French for gherkin, a very small variety of cucumber. Pickled, cornichons are a traditional accompaniment to pâté.

egg some recipes in this book call for raw or barely cooked eggs; exercise caution if there is a salmonella problem in your area.

fish sauce called naam pla on the label if it is Thai made; the Vietnamese version, nuoc naam, is almost identical. Made from pulverised salted fermented fish (most often anchovies); has a pungent smell and strong taste. There are many versions of varying intensity, so use sparingly.

flour
  plain an all-purpose flour, made from wheat.
  self-raising plain flour sifted with baking powder in the proportion of 1 cup flour to 2 teaspoons baking powder.

focaccia a flat Italian-style bread.

ginger also known as green or root ginger; the thick gnarled root of a tropical plant.

golden syrup a by-product of refined sugarcane; pure maple syrup or honey can be substituted.

hoisin sauce a thick, sweet and spicy chinese paste made from salted fermented soy beans, onions and garlic.

hummus a Middle Eastern dip made from softened dried chickpeas, garlic, lemon juice and tahini (sesame seed paste); can be purchased from most delicatessens and supermarkets.

kumara Polynesian name of orange-fleshed sweet potato often confused with yam.

lavash bread flat, unleavened bread of Mediterranean origin.

lebanese cucumber small and thin-skinned; it is also known as the european or burpless cucumber.

mayonnaise we prefer to use whole egg mayonnaise in our recipes.

mortadella a delicately spiced and smoked italian sausage made of pork and beef.

muesli also known as granola.

oil

olive made from ripened olives. *Extra virgin* and *virgin* are the first and second press, respectively. *Extra light* or *light* refers to taste, not fat levels.

vegetable any of a number of oils sourced from plants rather than animal fats.

onions

brown and white are interchangeable. Their pungent flesh adds flavour to a vast range of dishes.

green also known as scallion or, incorrectly, shallot; an immature onion picked before the bulb has formed, having a long, bright-green edible stalk.

red onion also known as red spanish, spanish or bermuda onion; a sweet-flavoured, large, purple-red onion, that is particularly good in salads.

orecchiette a small, round, donut-shaped pasta.

paprika ground dried red capsicum (bell pepper), available sweet, hot or smoked.

pine nuts also known as pignoli; not, in fact, a nut but a small, cream-coloured kernel from pine cones.

pitta also known as lebanese bread. This wheat-flour pocket bread is sold in large, flat pieces that separate into two thin rounds. Smaller, pocket pitta is also available.

polenta also known as cornmeal; a flour-like cereal made of dried corn (maize) sold ground in several different textures; also the name of the dish made from it.

puff pastry, ready-rolled packaged sheets of frozen puff pastry, which are available from supermarkets.

refried beans pinto beans, cooked twice (soaked and boiled, then mashed and fried). A Mexican staple, frijoles refritos, or refried beans, are available canned in supermarkets.

rice paper sheets also known as banh trang. Are made from rice paste and store well at room temperature. Are brittle and will break if dropped; must be dipped in warm water before using.

risoni also known as risi; small, rice-shaped pasta very similar to another small pasta, orzo.

rocket also known as arugula, rugula and rucola; a peppery-tasting green leaf that can be used similarly to baby spinach leaves. *Baby rocket leaves* are both smaller and less peppery.

rolled oats oat groats (oats that have been husked) that have been steamed-softened, flattened and dried.

sambal oelek (also ulek or olek) Indonesian in origin; a salty paste made from ground chillies and vinegar.

semi-dried tomatoes partially dried tomato pieces in olive oil; are softer and juicier than sun-dried, however, do not keep as long as sun-dried.

snow peas also called mange tout ('eat all'). *Snow pea tendrils*, the growing shoots of the plant, are sold by green grocers.

tomato

canned whole peeled tomatoes in natural juices

cherry also known as tiny tim or tom thumb tomatoes, small and round.

egg also called plum or roma, smallish, oval-shaped tomatoes much used salads.

paste a triple-concentrated tomato puree.

pasta sauce a commercially-prepared sauce usually eaten with pasta.

puree canned pureed tomatoes (not tomato paste). Substitute with fresh peeled and pureed tomatoes.

sun-dried we used sun-dried tomatoes packaged in oil, unless otherwise specified.

tortillas round, unleavened thin bread originating in Mexico; can be made at home or purchased frozen, fresh or vacuum-packed. Two kinds are available, one made from wheat flour and the other from corn.

turkish bread also known as pide. Comes in long (about 45cm) flat loaves as well as individual rounds; made from wheat flour and sprinkled with sesame or black onion seeds.

tzatziki Greek yogurt and cucumber dish sometimes containing mint and/or garlic.

wholegrain mustard also known as seeded. A coarse-grain mustard made from crushed mustard seeds and dijon-style french mustard.

index

conversion chart

MEASURES

One Australian metric measuring cup holds approximately 250ml, one Australian metric tablespoon holds 20ml, one Australian metric teaspoon holds 5ml.

The difference between one country's measuring cups and another's is within a two- or three-teaspoon variance, and will not affect your cooking results. North America, New Zealand and the United Kingdom use a 15ml tablespoon.

All cup and spoon measurements are level. The most accurate way of measuring dry ingredients is to weigh them. When measuring liquids, use a clear glass or plastic jug with the metric markings.

We use large eggs with an average weight of 60g.

DRY MEASURES

METRIC	IMPERIAL
15g	½oz
30g	1oz
60g	2oz
90g	3oz
125g	4oz (¼lb)
155g	5oz
185g	6oz
220g	7oz
250g	8oz (½lb)
280g	9oz
315g	10oz
345g	11oz
375g	12oz (¾lb)
410g	13oz
440g	14oz
470g	15oz
500g	16oz (1lb)
750g	24oz (1½lb)
1kg	32oz (2lb)

LIQUID MEASURES

METRIC	IMPERIAL
30ml	1 fluid oz
60ml	2 fluid oz
100ml	3 fluid oz
125ml	4 fluid oz
150ml	5 fluid oz (¼ pint/1 gill)
190ml	6 fluid oz
250ml	8 fluid oz
300ml	10 fluid oz (½ pint)
500ml	16 fluid oz
600ml	20 fluid oz (1 pint)
1000ml (1 litre)	1¾ pints

LENGTH MEASURES

METRIC	IMPERIAL
3mm	⅛in
6mm	¼in
1cm	½in
2cm	¾in
2.5cm	1in
5cm	2in
6cm	2½in
8cm	3in
10cm	4in
13cm	5in
15cm	6in
18cm	7in
20cm	8in
23cm	9in
25cm	10in
28cm	11in
30cm	12in (1ft)

OVEN TEMPERATURES

These oven temperatures are only a guide for conventional ovens. For fan-forced ovens, check the manufacturer's manual.

	°C (CELSIUS)	°F (FAHRENHEIT)	GAS MARK
Very slow	120	250	½
Slow	150	275 – 300	1 – 2
Moderately slow	170	325	3
Moderate	180	350 – 375	4 – 5
Moderately hot	200	400	6
Hot	220	425 – 450	7 – 8
Very hot	240	475	9

Are you missing some of the world's favourite cookbooks

The Australian Women's Weekly cookbooks are available from bookshops, cookshops, supermarkets and other stores all over the world. You can also buy direct from the publisher, using the order form below.

MINI SERIES £3.50 190x138MM 64 PAGES

TITLE	QTY	TITLE	QTY	TITLE	QTY
4 Fast Ingredients		Curries		Noodles	
15-minute Feasts		Drinks		Outdoor Eating	
30-minute Meals		Fast Fish		Party Food	
50 Fast Chicken Fillets		Fast Food for Friends		Pasta	
After-work Stir-fries		Fast Soup		Pickles and Chutneys	
Barbecue		Finger Food		Potatoes	
Barbecue Chicken		Gluten-free Cooking		Risotto	
Barbecued Seafood		Healthy Everyday Food 4 Kids		Roast	
Biscuits, Brownies & Biscotti		Ice-creams & Sorbets		Salads	
Bites		Indian Cooking		Simple Slices	
Bowl Food		Indonesian Favourites		Simply Seafood	
Burgers, Rösti & Fritters		Italian		Skinny Food	
Cafe Cakes		Italian Favourites		Stir-fries	
Cafe Food		Jams & Jellies		Summer Salads	
Casseroles		Kids Party Food		Tapas, Antipasto & Mezze	
Char-grills & Barbecues		Last-minute Meals		Thai Cooking	
Cheesecakes, Pavlovas & Trifles		Lebanese Cooking		Thai Favourites	
Chinese Favourites		Low Fat Fast		The Packed Lunch	
Chocolate Cakes		Malaysian Favourites		Vegetarian	
Christmas Cakes & Puddings		Mince Favourites		Vegetarian Stir-fries	
Cocktails		Mince		Vegie Main Meals	
Crumbles & Bakes		Muffins		Wok	
				TOTAL COST	£

Photocopy and complete coupon below

Name _____

Address _____

_____ Postcode _____

Country _____ Phone (business hours) _____

Email*(optional) _____
* By including your email address, you consent to receipt of any email regarding this magazine, and other emails which inform you of ACP's other publications, products, services and events, and to promote third party goods and services you may be interested in.

I enclose my cheque/money order for £ _____ or please charge £ _____

to my: ☐ Access ☐ Mastercard ☐ Visa ☐ Diners Club
   PLEASE NOTE: WE DO NOT ACCEPT SWITCH OR ELECTRON CARDS

Card number | | | | | | | | | | | | | | | | |

3 digit security code *(found on reverse of card)* _____

Cardholder's signature _____ Expiry date ____ /____

To order: Mail or fax – photocopy or complete the order form above, and send your credit card details or cheque/money order to: Australian Consolidated Press (UK), Moulton Park Business Centre, Red House Road, Moulton Park, Northampton NN3 6AQ, phone (+44) (01) 604 497531, fax (+44) (01) 604 497533, e-mail books@acpmedia.co.uk. Or order online at www.acpuk.com.
Non-UK residents: We accept the credit cards listed on the coupon, or cheques, drafts or International Money Orders payable in sterling and drawn on a UK bank. Credit card charges are at the exchange rate current at the time of payment.
All pricing current at time of going to press and subject to change/availability.
Postage and packing UK: Add £1.00 per order plus 25p per book.
Postage and packing overseas: Add £2.00 per order plus 50p per book. **Offer ends 31.12.2006**